Made in United States
North Haven, CT
13 October 2024

58723542R00071